Reboot Your Finances

Rethink Spending and Get Your Money Back on Track

Paul Andrew Smith

Copyright © 2020 by Paul Andrew Smith

The right of Paul Andrew Smith to be identified as the author of this book has been asserted by him in accordance with the Copyright, Designs and Patents Act 1988.

All rights reserved. No part of this publication may be reproduced, distributed, or transmitted in any form or by any means, including photocopying, recording, or other electronic or mechanical methods, without the prior written permission of the publisher, except in the case of brief quotations embodied in critical reviews and certain other non-commercial uses permitted by copyright law. For permission requests, write to the copyright owner or publisher.

CONTENTS

INTRODUCTION 1

The Basics - Personal Money Matters 3

Avoid ATM Overspending 9

Use Credit Cards Wisely (or Not at All)..................11

Make Use of Employer Benefits 17

Charitable Contributions Not in the Budget........19

The Lottery, Scratch-offs, and Gambling 22

Foreign Exchange and Fees 24

Improve Earning Potential with Education............25

Consider Quality Online Courses.............................27

Manage Home, Transportation, and Utility Costs...............29

Mortgage or Rent – The Cost of Having a Home 30

Save on Utility Services 35

Managing Cellphone Costs..40

Home Maintenance and Renovations 44

Do Not Buy Brand-New Cars Ever..........................48

Avoid Insurance You Do Not Need.........................52

Better Gas Mileage and Saving on Fuel................55

- Avoid Expensive Tickets and Fines 58
- Wash and Detail Your Own Vehicles 60
- Raising Children on a Budget 61
- Quality Care for Pets with Minimal Expense 64
- Stop Buying Food You Do Not Eat 67
- The Modern Plague of Bottled Water 70
- Daily Coffee or Other Beverage Purchases 72
- Cooking for Yourself Saves More Money 74
- Convenience Store Purchases Cost You More 77
- Smart Shopping Tips to Save More 79
- Cash Back, Points and Gift Card Opportunities 82
- Thrift Store Shopping and Second-hand Goods 87
- Brand Names Do Not Mean Higher Value 89
- Save More with Low Unit Prices 91
- Save on Holidays Without Being a Grinch 94
- Forget Paying for Entertainment Media 95
- Phones and Digital Connectivity 97
- Kitchen and Household Gadgets 99
- Fitness for Both Body and Finances 101

Break Addictions and Minimize Vices 103

Make Socializing More Affordable 104

Frugal Options for Fun and Personal Care 106

Spending Decisions for Your Wedding 107

Beauty Products and Appearances 109

Hobbies – Saving Money on Favorite Pastimes 111

Congratulations 114

INTRODUCTION

How do you feel when you look at your bank account balance at the end of every month? No matter how much money you earn, you can still find yourself in the trap of living paycheck to paycheck. This leads to unnecessary stress, unexpected bills turning into financial emergencies, and long-term plans getting pushed further and further into the realm of "maybe one day." You need to reboot your finances and shift the way you use your money to live a more comfortable and dream-filled life. The easiest way to start the process of getting your finances back on track involves a reduction in spending across the board. When you create a budget and track where your money comes from and where it goes, you will have more control and freedom at the same time. Chances are you do not currently have a strong understanding of your personal financial status. The convenience of direct payments leads to mindless expenditures. Forgotten subscriptions make your bank accounts spring a leak every month. Lack of understanding about the big topics like mortgages, car insurance and credit translate into problems very quickly. As you read this book, you will learn many ways to do exactly what the title says: "Reboot Your Finances." In every section, find ways to hold on to more money and make it work for you. It all starts with a working budget, an intelligent plan for spending less and a healthy dose of self-control.

The Basics - Personal Money Matters

The first step in any financial transformation involves creating a budget. Unless you do this, you have little chance of gaining control of your money. While suggestions to give up takeout lunch or turn your thermostat lower in the winter help save you money, if you do not keep track of anything, how do you know if it is really making a difference?

Build a Budget to Understand Your Financial Foundation

You do not need any fancy accounting software or banking apps to create a budget. However, these things can help keep you organized and on track. All you really need is some type of list or chart that shows where your money comes from and where it goes on a monthly basis. For best results, track everything for three or four months to get an accurate picture of your entire financial truth.

Income and Other Earnings

When a paycheck, bonus, tips, business revenue or any other type of income goes into your wallet or bank, write it down. This is the maximum amount of money you can spend. If taxes are not taken out of the income before it hits your accounts, make sure you only write down your net income after you take care of the government's percentage.

Every Single Expense

Write dates and amounts for scheduled bills, regular expenses, and incidental purchases like gas for your car or the caramel macchiato you had a craving for on the way home from work. Be honest and thorough if you want to truly rework your financial truth and make a positive difference in your life. Now that you understand where your money comes from and goes, you can begin to rethink your spending and get everything on a better track to a brighter future. To do that, read the rest of the book and put these tips and techniques into practice in your everyday life.

Keep Track of Bank Accounts

It makes sense to look online regularly to check for unexpected transactions on your checking and savings account statements. This helps you keep an eye out for over-billing, unexpected fees or fraudulent activity. The last thing you want is to throw away your hard-earned money or have someone steal it from you through identity theft or similar issues.

Besides watching your own funds, however, paying attention to changes in the account rules also make sense. Banks change hands and rules semi-frequently, and the free checking account you signed up for last year may morph into a fee-based one with only a small print mailer to tell you of any change. Shop around for different accounts to prevent your income from being chipped away by unnecessary fees. All fees are not created equal, however. In some cases, and based on your lifestyle and regular purchases, a fee may get you special benefits that will save you money in the long run. Weigh the pros and cons to determine whether the value of the perks outweigh the total fee amount.

Three banking options to consider include:

Online High-yield Accounts

Although interest rates on ordinary checking or savings accounts will not make you rich, there is no reason to ignore a potential source of additional income. Online banks offer all the security and most of the convenience of bricks-and-mortar branches with considerably higher APRs.

Sign Up Bonuses

If you intend to switch to a different banking establishment, shop around for companies that give free money when you sign up and complete a few transactions. You can earn $100 or more by using direct deposit or your debit card for a specific number of purchases.

Cash Back or Points Debit Cards

Some banks offer direct financial benefits whenever you use their ATM or debit card to make a withdrawal or a purchase. Getting a penny or two back on every dollar you spend may not sound like a big deal, however it can add up over time and improve your overall financial standing. You can frequently exchange earned points for gift cards and similar prizes.

No matter which bank you choose or how you use it to pay your bills and other expenses, the most important rule of improving your finances is to pay attention. Keep writing everything in your budget and set up automated payments to ensure the necessary bills are covered no matter what.

Avoid ATM Overspending

A bank account that offers cashback or points every time you use your debit card sounds great, but that does not mean you should whip it out every time you need some cash. ATMs offer convenience and easy access but come with multiple hidden dangers that can destroy your budget quickly.

Always use a cash machine provided by your bank, specifically if you want to avoid fees. If you have an account at a regional or national bank, you should be able to find a branch near your location. If you use another bank or one of the non-affiliated ATMs located at another establishment, you may find multiple charges against your bank account.

Never Pay an ATM Fee

The ATM itself may charge $2 – $3 for a transaction. Your bank or the holder of your debit card may also charge an additional fee for using it at a non-approved machine. Does it make sense to pay $3.00 or more just to have some cash in your wallet? In our increasingly cashless society, it is exceedingly rare that you will need some anyway. You can swipe or tap your debit card to pay directly at most shops, gas stations, restaurants, and other businesses. They work just like a credit card when shopping online. The best way to avoid these fees completely is to plan ahead. If you want to have cash on hand, simply withdraw some from your bank account when you make a deposit or by heading to a branch directly. Chances are those bills will sit in your wallet ready for an emergency.

Use Credit Cards Wisely (or Not at All)

Nothing messes up your financial future faster than using excessive amounts of credit and going into debt because you cannot pay it all back right away. In the early months of 2020, the US Federal Reserve revealed that Americans as a whole owe over $930 billion worth of credit card debt. That is nearly $3000 for every man, woman and child living in this country. A credit card's purpose makes sense. It gives you an option to pay for things in a convenient and secure way without carrying cash in your pocket. It allows you to cover unexpected emergencies even if you do not have enough money on hand. For these reasons alone, it makes sense to have one or two cards you can use if necessary. They provide protection and peace of mind.

However, as indicated by the ridiculous debt numbers mentioned above, they also provide headaches, massive amounts of stress and financial ruin for people who misuse them.

Avoiding Debt Is Your #1 Priority

To manage your finances properly, never use a credit card to pay for anything you cannot afford to cover by the end of the month. The moment you leave a balance on the card beyond the payment due date, interest charges get tacked on to your total debt. Failure to pay on time diminishes your credit score, racks up additional fees and sucks you down in a credit/debt whirlpool that is nearly impossible to escape from.

These simple organizational rules will save you:

- Use your credit card only when you can afford to.

- Pay back the full amount on time every month.
- Avoid using credit cards with annual fees or other account charges.
- Do not use all of your available credit. Keep charges low.
- Mark down all purchases and payments in your monthly budget.

These guidelines not only leave you in control of your finances but also help improve your credit score. This magical number is necessary for everything from getting a good rate on a car loan to renting an apartment to getting a job in some cases.

If You Have Debt Already

Pay it off as quickly as possible. With all the money you will save by following the advice in this book, you can add to your monthly payments and get rid of credit card debt sooner than you imagine.

Avoid Consults and Consolidation

Most US citizens carry some type of debt. This can range from a simple and responsible mortgage to massive, uncontrollable credit card charges that have snowballed due to interest and fees. Any type of debt can cause stress and a feeling that you will never get out from these financial shackles. If you have more than one debt, the situation becomes even more complex. Juggling payment plans, figuring out where to put any extra money you earn and creating a repayment schedule can leave you with a lot of confusion and worry. Shiny advertisements for credit consultations and debt consolidation loans may seem very attractive; after all, they promise help and sometimes claim you will end up paying back less than you actually owe.

The first thing to realize is that anytime you bring in the so-called experts, they will need payment for their services. Consultations and consolidation both carry fees of some kind. Debt consolidation loans may give you just one payment every month, but the interest rate may exceed what you are currently paying. Why would you want to pay extra for things that you can take care of yourself? Why would you want to end up paying more than you must?

Keep Costs as Low as Possible

Free help exists online and through consumer organizations. Study trusted sources to learn how to handle multiple debts intelligently. The best way to avoid the stress of money issues is to understand what is going on and take action to make it better. Paying off debt is a lot like making a budget. Follow these steps to consolidate your own financial problems and chip away at them in an effective manner.

1 – Write down every debt holder, amount, minimum payment, payment date, and interest rate.

2 – Put the payment dates on your calendar or scheduling app with the minimum payment indicated. No matter what, you must pay this amount before the bill is due.

3 – Organize your debts with the highest interest rate on top. Pay off this debt first to minimize the overall cost of interest for the long term. While paying the minimum on all bills, put any extra money you get on this first debt until it is gone.

4 – Once one debt is repaid, snowball its total payment into the next highest interest rate. Continue this until you are free.

Make Use of Employer Benefits

Unfortunately, far too many companies and organizations get out of giving employee benefits by only hiring part-time workers or using other loopholes in the system. No matter where you work, the hours you keep or your payment arrangement, take time to investigate whether you are eligible for any benefits. These may include paid time off work, holiday allowances, healthcare, retirement funds or more unusual perks, like use of an on-site fitness center or childcare.

The more you know, the more you may save. For example, some companies offer healthcare savings if you take part in their wellness programs or lunch hour walking club. These savings add up over time and improve your health, which also saves you money on everything from doctor's visits to snacks at the vending machine. If you have a child, using company babysitting or preschool can save you hundreds of dollars every month.

Other possible employee benefits may include the use of a company vehicle, discounted transportation tickets for your commute, products or services that the company itself provides for less or use of computer hardware or other devices. Always follow the rules but take advantage of any perks available to you.

Charitable Contributions Not in the Budget

As much as contributing to one of the thousands of nonprofit organizations in the world makes you feel emotionally fulfilled, you still need to budget these expenditures. You may feel a strong pull to support human rights, animal care, environmental activism, or any other type of important cause. Like they tell you during the safety instructions before an airplane flight, you must put your own mask on first before helping someone next to you.

If you currently carry debt or have trouble making ends meet, now is not the time to give away your hard-earned money. Do not add extra pressure to your personal finance out of generosity that you cannot afford. There are other ways to support charities and causes that will not affect your ability to pay your bills, overcome debt or save for retirement.

Other Ways to Pay It Forward

1 – If you currently donate on a monthly or quarterly basis, cancel the automatic payments. If you receive a bonus at work or an unexpected monetary gift, you may consider donating a portion of it to your favorite cause.

2 – Donate time instead of money. Tons of different volunteer opportunities exist that will not cost you anything except some gas in your car to get to the location. Consider signing up for walks or runs and raise money through your efforts.

3 – Volunteer your special skills. If you play the piano, spend an hour or two sharing your musical talent with seniors at an assisted living facility. If you have a keen sense for event organization, get involved with fundraising events.

4 – Share unwanted yet high-quality goods. Many charitable organizations accept clothing, furniture,

toys, books, and other items to either distribute to the less fortunate or to sell in thrift shops.

You will feel wonderful because you are still contributing to the causes you care about but best of all, you will not add money worries and stress to your own plate at the same time.

The Lottery, Scratch-offs, and Gambling

Those stories in the news about someone becoming an overnight millionaire lure nearly 90 million people to purchase a lottery ticket every year in the United States. Yet with how few winners there are annually, you are actually far more likely to be struck by lightning or killed by bees than purchase a winning ticket.

The lottery, scratch off tickets and all other types of gambling are a type of fantasy that do not provide nearly as much entertainment as watching a movie or reading a book. If you travel to Las Vegas or Atlantic City to gamble with friends on vacation, at least you are getting something else out of it; a hotel stay, restaurant meals and a few shows. What pleasure do you really get from scratching off a ticket only to find out you have lost once again?

These distractions have no place in a regular budget. They give you an extremely short thrill that usually ends in negativity. It is a complete waste of money that has virtually no chance of reward.

Foreign Exchange and Fees

Of the 330 million-plus Americans, only around 20 million of them own a passport. International travel is expensive, takes more time than the average person has off work every year and is simply not in the budget for many people. However, if you do travel outside the country for work or pleasure, it is feasible to save on foreign currency exchange fees if you plan ahead and make wise decisions. If possible, exchange currencies stateside before you leave. If not, find a local bank or ATM with the lowest fees.

Your best options for using foreign currency include:

- Fee-free debit or credit cards from online banks
- International allowances from your existing credit card
- Pre-paid currency cards

Improve Earning Potential with Education

Creating a workable budget, choosing the best bank accounts and credit cards and paying off debt as quickly as possible are all important parts of rebooting your finances. However, instead of just watching your spending, learn how to increase your income or future earning potential.

Undoubtedly, education is the best way to earn more money in the long run. The US Bureau of Labor Statistics determined that people with high school diplomas earn a median income of just under $36,000 annually. A bachelor's degree gives you a median income over $59,000. A PhD recipient has median yearly pay over $84,000. The ranges surrounding those totals vary widely, however it is easy to see that training and skills make you more marketable and valuable to the workforce. Temper those income levels with student loan debts. Nearly 70% of all college graduates carry an average of $30,000 in debt. Is that worth the potential boost in earnings? More importantly, is there another way for you to improve your education and marketability without going into so much debt?

Ways to Get a Free Education

There are very few ways to get an advanced education or training free in the United States:

- Federal, state, local, or specific grants
- Scholarships based on merit or need
- US Military programs
- Employment at a school in rare cases
- Apprenticeships for some trades
- Tuition reimbursement from your employer

Consider Quality Online Courses

You will not get a bachelors, masters or doctorate degree from online tutorials and lessons. While you can attend virtual colleges, you must pay for them just like any other brick-and-mortar school.

However free or low-cost online courses can teach you marketable skills that help you boost your income. Potential earners like website or graphic design, programming, writing, Internet marketing and other professional and creative endeavors can work for you if you dedicate your time and energy to gaining excellent skills.

Unfortunately, all classes are not created equal. Never pay for something before you fully explore free options. Double check resources and lessons to make sure they are accurate and up to date. Research the instructors to make sure they really know what they are talking about.

Do not waste your time just because something is free. The classic adage, "Time is money" is true. Building a sought-after skill set can help you get promotions at your current job, find a new one or start your own self-employment or entrepreneurial adventure.

You have already learnt know how to start a basic budget, avoid some of the common pitfalls associated with managing your money, pay off your debt as quickly as possible and even boost your income. Now it is time to reboot your thinking and dive into specific choices and actions that will change your financial future for the better.

Manage Home, Transportation, and Utility Costs

Food, shelter, transportation and utilities like electricity and heat should top your list of needs every month. These take up the bulk of your income and you cannot avoid paying the bills unless you want serious problems on your hands.

The following topics will help you manage your mortgage or rent, monthly utility bills, car insurance, gasoline budget, and more. If you truly want to reboot your finances, changing how much you pay for these necessary things matters so much more than giving up a daily latte or clipping coupons before every shopping trip.

Mortgage or Rent – The Cost of Having a Home

The first question to consider is whether it costs less overall to purchase a house or to rent an apartment or condo. The answer to this question depends on so many factors that it is difficult to come up with one answer. To figure this out, you need to consider many issues including:

- Your credit score and resulting interest rates
- Local cost-of-living
- The size of your needed home
- Extra expenses such as maintenance and yard care
- If you plan to stay nearby for a long time
- …and so many more.

The goal of this book is not to help you determine what works best for you. Instead, learn how to minimize your expenses for either of them so you do not waste money or get caught in a debt that you have no hope of repaying.

Save on Your Mortgage

The median cost for a home in the United States is $226,000. The actual price of a home depends on size, condition and mostly geographic location. In a pleasant West Virginia suburb, you can easily purchase a three-bedroom home for around $105,000. In California, the same simple house would cost $568,000. Most people need to buy a house near the location of their job and may not have a lot of options. In any state or city, you can still save money on your mortgage if you shop around and make wise decisions. Far too many people buy more house than they could afford and end up suffering for the next 15 or 30 years. Getting forced into foreclosure is even worse.

1 – Get the highest credit score you possibly can before you apply for mortgages. This will get you more approvals at lower interest rates.

2 – Shop around with different banks, credit unions and mortgage lenders for the best deals possible. Before you apply, understand how much house you can truly afford.

3 – Consider a fixed rate mortgage for steadier payments that will not surprise you if the economy experiences extreme fluctuations. You always have the option to refinance down the road if it makes sense.

Once you have an appropriate mortgage and move into your new home, pay the whole bill off as soon as possible. Those monthly bills continue for 15, 30, or even more years and include a massive amount of interest over the life of the loan. To minimize the total amount you end up paying, submit bi-weekly payments and put extra money on the principle whenever possible.

Choosing a Reasonable Rent

Comfort matters, but if you are not financially comfortable, saving money matters more. The ideal apartment is as small as you can stand it, at a convenient location to your job to minimize commute time and expenses, in a safe part of town with accessible shops and services and with a professional management team who keeps things in good repair. To minimize your rent, consider moving in with a friend or advertising for a roommate. Always make sure you can cover the full rent on your own to prevent credit-destroying evictions or other issues if the roommate leaves suddenly.

Save on Utility Services

If you rent instead of owning your own home, you may find available apartments or condominiums with included utilities, most frequently heating and hot water. However, they can also include high-speed Internet in some cases. Because every household uses a different amount of electricity, you will have to handle that bill all on your own.

If you own a home, you are responsible for all utility bills and choices. Use as little as possible; you can learn more about reducing these bills in the section on energy efficiency later in this book.

Choose the Best Suppliers

You may not realize you can manage your services to minimize spending, even before you consider turning all the lights off or keeping the heat at 60 degrees and wearing three sweaters and a woolly hat indoors all winter long. In most places around the country, you have the right to choose different utility suppliers. Electricity or natural gas works the same no matter which company you get from. The differences include rates, fees and services such as the maintenance.

Shop around for introductory rates offered to new customers. Switching to a different electricity company does not involve rewiring your whole house or any invasive procedures at all. Therefore, it is quite simple to contact the company and change things over. However, do be aware of contract terms associated with the lower rate or fee waivers; you do not want to get locked into higher charges.

Submit Usage Information Monthly

If a meter reader does not come to your house or you do not submit your own information through their convenient online portals, the utility company will estimate your bill. This can force you to pay extra that you don't owe. Of course, they will readjust as soon as they get an accurate reading, but you will not have access to your money in the meantime.

Improve Energy Efficiency and Save

Every time you turn on a lamp, fire up your computer, plug in an electric skillet, take a shower or run the air conditioner, you use up electricity or other energy sources like natural gas or oil. Switching suppliers only goes so far. Ultimately you should use energy efficiently in order to save money. When you rethink how much you spend on the smallest everyday activities, you can make a real difference in your monthly bills. Before you get nervous about massive lifestyle changes or living your life in the dark or cold, this is not an extreme frugality book. You can make virtually unnoticeable changes based on mindfulness that help improve your overall budget and give you some extra money for paying off debt, adding to retirement savings or spending on fun.

Temperature Control

Turning up the thermostat is not the only way to make your home warmer; doing that will only increase your bills. Instead, consider a long-term investment in better windows, more sealant, extra insulation in the walls, or something as simple as thicker curtains, draft excluders and insulating storm doors.

Once you improve energy efficiency in these ways, then it becomes time to put on an extra sweater and buy yourself some fuzzy slippers at the next sale.

Save on Electricity

The only way to minimize your electricity bill is to use less. You cannot make one kilowatt hour power more devices; instead only use what you truly need. Turn off lights in favor of natural sunlight through the windows. Replace bulbs with long-lasting LED options. Turn off or unplug hardly used items like digital clocks, decorations, and the numerous kitchen gadgets you bought but never really use. None of these things will negatively affect your comfort or lifestyle but they will reduce your monthly bill so you can manage debt, build up a greater emergency fund and finally realize peace of mind from your financial woes.

Managing Cellphone Costs

Everyone has a smartphone these days. In fact, on a global scale, 95% of people everywhere own one. In many cases, they have completely replaced landline telephones as the primary form of communication for both business and personal purposes. Telling someone not to get a cellphone in order to save money makes no sense in today's world. Not only do you need a mobile phone, you also need one that provides access to the Internet and powers the wide variety of apps available for use.

Far too many people focus on trends, innovation, or image when it comes to choosing a phone, a service plan and all the extras. Part of rebooting your thinking about personal finance includes a shift in your purchasing mindset. Chasing trends or buying this year's phone when last year's still works fine is one of the ideas you must eradicate from your life.

Inexpensive Phones Work Just as Well

Basic smartphones exist for less than $100. On the other hand, you could purchase the latest iPhone or other model for nearly $2000. Besides status from having a hot brand name in your pocket, what is the real difference in how the gadgets function? Yes, some models are faster, more powerful, have more storage space and come with more functions than others. The most important consideration is what you really need to be able to do everything you want. The average person makes calls, texts people, accesses social media, uses a few apps for shopping or research and maybe uses their phone for some work purposes; almost any phone can do these things without a problem.

Besides choosing a phone that costs 25% or even 50% less than the hottest brands, keep using the same phone until it is truly obsolete or does not work anymore. Upgrading every year simply makes no sense.

Saving on Service Plans

Shop around for service before going with your local utility company. Do not pay for access or data levels that you never use. Unlimited everything is quite affordable these days. Consider off-brand options like Ting or Mint to pay less than $10 per month. For many people, prepaid phones or pay-as-you-go plans work well. This is the best way to spend money on what you use instead of what the companies think you want.

All the Accessories You Do Not Need

Another way to save money on your phone purchases and usage is to avoid buying accessories that provide no real benefits. A phone case and screen protector make sense; for an incredibly low cost, they help protect your gadget from falls and scratches. A $20 one works just as well as the $100 model. Also, ask yourself this: do you really need five different types of chargers, specialty phone earbuds, speakers, a branded pop socket or high-tech car mount?

Home Maintenance and Renovations

If you own a home, maintaining it takes a lot of time and regular expenditures to keep everything looking and functioning well. Of course, things like cleaning and fixing appliances or other things that break need to be constantly monitored. Other home projects, such as do-it-yourself improvements or professional remodeling and renovation tasks, require a different approach. Before you start calling contractors, take a close look at your budget.

Keep Regular Maintenance Costs Down

Something as simple as purchasing generic cleaning solutions and using rags instead of high-tech sponges to scrub your surfaces helps you save money. This may be a paradigm shift for some shoppers who have always reached for brand names and the latest products. In the end, elbow grease cleans more than any specialty gadget or solution on the market today. Also, inexpensive things like white vinegar, simple soap powder and basic mops and brooms are better for the environment.

Save on Repairs – Is DIY a Good Choice?

Many homeowners immediately think that do-it-yourself repairs and improvements will save them money. This is only true if you actually know what you are doing. Far too many self-proclaimed experts end up making things worse or leaving a half-finished project that requires professional help to complete. If you have reasonable handiness skills, you can learn how to do almost anything by watching a YouTube video or looking at photos in a tutorial. This is a great way to save money for things like changing a showerhead or installing a window covering. Leave major plumbing, electrical work and building projects to the experts.

Renovation and Remodeling Projects

If you do want to change the interior or exterior of your home in a more extreme way, getting multiple price quotes for renovation and remodeling projects is a must. First ask yourself if the change is necessary? Ask if it will increase property value in the long term? Finally, figure out what a reasonable budget is for the entire thing. If you can, only make changes you can afford without taking out a home loan or using credit as that will drastically increase the overall price.

How do you find affordable service providers? Start with online research. Do not skimp on quality by hiring someone under the table, without insurance or with questionable testimonials from former clients. That only leads to the potential for financial ruin if something goes wrong. Work with professionals to come up with a smart plan for the renovation or remodeling process. Remember that you can tackle some finishing work or details on your own to save money. For example, if you want to have a fence installed, consider letting the professionals build it but painting it on your own.

Do Not Buy Brand-New Cars Ever

Americans love their cars, which has led to a belief that buying a new car is a symbol of having arrived or achieving success. When success comes with an excessively high price tag and provides no real value over buying a preowned car, in reality it makes little sense. Let go of the mindset that is drilled into the collective US culture to escape an expensive choice you do not have to make.

New cars depreciate so quickly that no one could ever consider them an investment. Why spend more money than you need to on something that will never allow you to recoup the cost? The new-car smell does not justify spending thousands unnecessarily.

Pay Cash for Cars Whenever Possible

One of the most important mental shifts anyone needs to make when they start thinking about smart budgeting involves the understanding that interest is evil. Any time you borrow money, you will end up needing to pay back more than you spent – interest is akin to a punishment for not saving up for things you need to buy before you head to the store. The only time it really makes sense to take out a car loan and make payments is if you are offered extraordinarily good terms. If you have an exceptionally high credit score, you may even get 0% financing. In that case, leave your money in an interest-bearing savings account or investment so it earns money while you pay just the principle on your car.

Do Not Lease Vehicles Either

Unless you get exceptional terms or only need a vehicle for a short amount of time, leasing makes less sense than buying a quality, previously owned car. Why pay interest and fees when you are not getting any of the perks of ownership? You cannot sell your leased car to recoup some of your expense when you are done using it.

How to Buy the Right Used Car

What kind of vehicle do you need? A young, single person who uses their car to commute and go out with friends on occasion does not need a massive SUV that gets low gas mileage and costs too much to insure. A family of five are likely to benefit more from a minivan than a sports car for mom and a pickup truck for dad.

Ask yourself these questions when choosing the right used car for you:

- How many people will ride in the car and how many seats do I need?

- Do I need to transport large or heavy loads frequently?
- What will insurance and maintenance cost for different types of vehicles?
- How much gas mileage does each option get?
- Does this type of car need specialty maintenance or have expensive repair charges?
- Am I buying this for practical use or as a status symbol?

Avoid Insurance You Do Not Need

You can buy insurance for almost anything these days from reasonable policies for your home or vehicles, to insurance for electronic gadgets and even your pet's teeth. Everyone who owns or rent a home should have insurance to cover the property or their belongings. If you have a mortgage, insurance is usually required by the lender. Everyone who owns a personal vehicle needs car or truck insurance too. In fact, this is legally required by most states in the country.

The easiest way to avoid paying too much for your monthly insurance bills is to cut out all unnecessary policies and coverage options. In the end, saving on any type of insurance is a matter of weighing up risk versus reward. You are essentially taking a gamble that nothing serious will happen. Since the chance of certain events is incredibly low, not paying for associated coverage makes sense.

Home or Renters Insurance Savings

These types of residence insurance policies cover everything from the structure itself to your belongings inside. Always read the fine print, determine what you can leave out and never double up on insurance. For example, if your home is not in a floodplain or you do not live in tornado alley, it makes little sense to get protection against these possibilities. If your insurance covers belongings inside the home, you don't also need separate insurance for your phone, big-screen TV or stamp collection.

Car Insurance Savings

Liability insurance offers the minimum protection accepted by law in most places. If you own your vehicle outright, you have the option to choose the cheapest policy possible. Cars with financing or leased vehicles, which are not a smart choice to begin with, may necessitate additional coverage. If you carry home and auto insurance with the same company, you may save money by bundling your services. Any time you raise your deductible, you do not have to pay as much for your monthly or annual bill. Always ask the issuing company about discounts. Realize that offers can change frequently, so you shouldn't decide on one policy and keep it forever without exploring the options. A good way to remind yourself to shop around involves paying your bill manually rather than setting up an auto subscription option.

Better Gas Mileage and Saving on Fuel

The number one way to save on gas for your vehicle starts before you make a purchase decision. When you buy a fuel-efficient car, the cost over time reduces drastically. Generally, the smaller the car, the less fuel it will need to take you from one place to the next. Consider a hybrid if you want to invest in eco-friendly transportation.

If you already have one or more vehicles and have no plans to trade them in anytime soon, you can still save on gas if you shop smart and drive defensively. The cost of gasoline changes all the time and varies a lot from one part of the country to another. In most cases you only have a few convenient gas stations to choose from when it comes time to fill up your car. If you do not have to drive out of your way, always choose the cheapest one. There is no reason to buy name-brand gasoline.

How to Save More on Gas Expenses

The following three driving tips will help you make the most of the gas you buy and will save you a lot of money over the lifetime of your car. These fundamental changes to where, when and how you drive represent the type of necessary rethinking of your spending habits you need to make.

1 – Only drive when and where you need to. Plan routes for convenience and avoid the scenic roads when you have more direct options. Why drive all the way home from work and then go out again to pick something up from the shop when you can stop at the shop in the path of your commute? Also, consider improving the environment and your health by walking or bicycling to nearby locations.

2 – Keep your car well-maintained. You can increase the efficiency of your vehicle's engine without taking it to a mechanic every month. Check the oil levels, pay attention to proper tire inflation and make sure there are no leaks or malfunctions. Also, avoid keeping a lot of clutter or heavy gear in the trunk or backseat. Extra weight uses more fuel.

3 – Drive smoothly and within the speed limit. When you obey the rules of the road, you minimize the chance of another big expense: traffic tickets. Driving within the speed limit also keeps your car working at maximum efficiency for the best gas mileage. Aggressive maneuvers like jackrabbit starts and rapid acceleration use more fuel than more relaxed driving habits.

Avoid Expensive Tickets and Fines

The average cost of a speeding ticket in the United States is $150. Other tickets for parking, ignoring road signs, running red lights, aggressive driving and using your cellphone can cost quite a bit more in some locations. You can avoid ever having to pay any type of driving ticket by always driving responsibly.

Far too many people believe that they get tickets and fines because the authorities have it out for motorists and need to fill some type of quota. When you reboot your thinking to take responsibility for your actions and your personal finance, you figure out that people get tickets and fines because they have done something wrong. Errors like speeding, failure to come to a complete stop at a STOP sign and parking illegally do not happen by accident. They are either due to negligence or simply not caring about following rules.

Traffic and related tickets not only cost a lot upfront, but they can also involve court costs and increases in your vehicle insurance payments. A quick one-off moment when you attempt to get away with illegal and potentially dangerous behavior can lead to a long period of increased expenses. If your bad driving decisions lead to an accident, you may experience even worse repercussions.

Wash and Detail Your Own Vehicles

A neat and shiny car looks great and may give you pride of ownership. Proper polishing and treatments may protect it from rust, corrosion due to road salts and other body damage. However, the automotive care industry has a huge number of different products you can use at home to get excellent results. Professional car washes and detailing services offer convenience, but they also represent an expense you do not need to add to your budget. Instead of paying approximately $10 for a basic carwash or up to $250 for a full detailing, get yourself a reusable bucket, a bottle of carwash solution, a sponge and a hose.

Owning a car or other vehicle does add more expenses to your budget. Minimizing them requires a shift in how you view your responsibility as a driver.

Raising Children on a Budget

Some sources state that it takes $1 million to raise a child from birth to the age of 18. While there is no doubt that having children adds extra expenses to your budget, you don't have to take things to such an extreme. A large part of providing for kids is making wise decisions that suit their needs and offer affordable ways to treat them occasionally. Society and other parents put a lot of pressure to spend a lot on things like birthday parties, toys and games and trips to places like Disney World.

A large part of any personal finance reboot is changing how you value different objects and experiences. Not only can you raise children well for less, but it also gives you the opportunity to teach them valuable lessons that can help them live a budget-friendly lifestyle when they become adults. This type of thing can prevent a lot of expectations and a sense of entitlement that some youngsters never outgrow.

Spend Money on the Important Things

Smart choices start at birth. Does a three-month-old need designer clothes and name-brand diapers? Does a toddler need a pair of shoes for every day of the week or just one sturdy pair that offers healthy foot support as they learn to walk? Will your child be happier with 20 presents under the Christmas tree, or would they enjoy a few carefully chosen ones just as much?

Good rules of thumb for spending money on children's things include:

- Buy classic clothes and toys instead of chasing trends.
- Do not spend money on things your child will never remember.

- Create experiences based on quality time instead of sparkle.
- Hand-me-downs, preowned toys and thrift store games work just as well.

Financial Literacy for Big Kids and Teens

One of the best gifts that a parent can give their child is the ability to understand money and the importance of working for what you need and want. Some parents decide to give a weekly allowance with no strings attached while others pay their sons and daughters to do chores or get good grades. Associating earned money with action makes more sense. Grade school children begin to learn about money and can practice using it wisely by saving up for special toys or games they want. Take an active role in teaching your kids how to manage their finances intelligently to prevent financial problems down the road.

Quality Care for Pets with Minimal Expense

For some people, owning a pet feels like a necessity rather than a luxury. If you do not have one yet, take a careful look at your budget to make sure you can afford one before inviting one to join your family. A full 85 million households in the United States own one or more pets. Responsible pet ownership requires spending money, but it may not be as expensive as you think.

You Can Save on Everyday Pet Care

Pets require four main things: veterinary care, food, shelter, and fun. Do not skimp on veterinary care. While you can shop around to find discount services, free rabies shot clinics and special offers on space and neuters, if your dog or cat is sick or injured, you must have money on hand to take them to the vet.

When it comes to food, opt for quality nutrition to prevent health problems and allergies. This does not mean you have to buy the most expensive branded kibble or cans. Compare ingredients and choose the least expensive, quality option. Your house provides the primary shelter for any pet. For birds, fish, reptiles or small furry animals like hamsters, the most important criteria include sufficient space and inability to escape. A used aquarium or birdcage you assemble yourself works just as well as a premium option available at a pet boutique. When it comes to fun, your pets may prefer interacting with you more than any high-tech gadget or toy. Pick up a pack of simple tennis balls or a stuffed mouse if they fit your budget, however pets can have just as much fun with a stick, a bottle or other free items.

Pet Expenses to Cut Out of the Budget

Pet culture in the USA has boosted the industry into the billions. People spend so much money on things such as gourmet chef-prepared dog food, diamond-studded cat collars and full-time nannies for their parrots. Obviously, none of these things are necessary to keep your pet healthy and happy.

Avoid these unnecessary expenses at the pet store:
- Pet clothing or costumes
- Luxury fabric collars and leashes
- Gourmet treats like dog biscuits and carrot cake for a pet rabbit
- Fancy grooming services – the tub and a towel work well enough!

Stop Buying Food You Do Not Eat

Twenty million tons of food is thrown out in the United States every year. The average household wastes approximately 30% of all the food they purchase. Not only is this a ridiculous problem for the environment and natural resources, it also destroys your grocery budget for no reason at all.

Buying food happens almost automatically for many people. You go to the supermarket and pick out groceries you know will make delicious meals and snacks but, unless you have a plan, a lot of that money will end up in the garbage. It isn't just a matter of produce going bad or moldy; how many times have you found a can of something that sat on the shelf for a year or a covered dish of some unidentifiable leftovers shoved to the very back of the fridge?

Adopt the Meal Plan Mindset

At a set time every week, sit down alone or with your family to devise a meal plan and grocery list. You know the meals you eat, or you can collect recipes to try for dinner every day. The most important thing is to determine how much of each ingredient you need and only buy that amount. Over time, this will help you create a pantry of staples with pasta, rice or other foods that lasts a long time on the shelf. People very rarely throw out uncooked rice, for example.

While some people cook all their meals on Sunday and package them for quick access throughout the week, you can easily store the ingredients in your fridge and freezer so they are still fresh if you prefer cooking every day. Bulk recipes using a crockpot or oven allows you to freeze portions so they will not spoil.

Shopping for Less Waste Overall

Fresh fruits and vegetables are the most common foods that go bad before you use them. Consider flash frozen options instead; frozen at the peak of freshness to maintain the nutrients.

Other options for saving money at the grocery store include only shopping sale items in planning your meals around that, using coupons and paying attention to unit price rather than package price. These can all make a big change in your grocery budget.

The Modern Plague of Bottled Water

Unfortunately, some places in the United States do not have healthy tap water. If you live in one of these areas, you either need to invest in a whole-house filtration system or purchase bottled water. In these cases, buying large bottles of generic brand water makes most financial sense.

However, most issues with bottled water are a matter of convenience. Not only do you pay 500 times the amount for water in a bottle than you do for water from the tap, you end up with tons of plastic pouring into the environment. Living frugally often equals living green.

Save Money on Drinking Water

One way to shift your budget when it comes to bottled water is to simply stop drinking it. While proper hydration is important, no one is going to dehydrate dangerously in an hour or two at the shop or office.

If you prefer to have water with you, pay a few dollars for a reusable bottle and fill it up from your tap at home before leaving the house. You can even add ice cubes or a slice of lemon or other fruit to improve the taste. Even with the expense of a lemon or two, you will still spend a fraction of the amount for your hydration habit.

Daily Coffee or Other Beverage Purchases

There is some criticism around the recommendation of giving up fancy coffee drinks in line with the overall state of the economy. While the memes make sense, you do not have the power to change the economy by yourself. You do however have the power to reboot your thinking and change your spending habits. A fancy coffee can cost as much as $5.00. Even a plain coffee at a popular chain is more than $2.00. A small black brew at a gas station or convenience store may only be $1.00 and you start to believe it's a great deal. However, if you brew a cup at home, you will only spend about $0.25.

Rethink Your Caffeine Fix

If you need to balance your budget, pay off a debt or save for a larger expense like a vacation, car, or retirement, making small changes in something as simple as coffee helps. Consider these cost savings over the course of a year:

Fancy coffee – $1825 from a shop vs. $180 at home

That gives you approximately an extra $138 per month, which can easily cover some utility bills or a week's worth of groceries. After saving that for 25 years, you will have an extra $41,000 plus interest from investing it to help fund your retirement.

Plain coffee – $730 vs. $92

While the savings from plain coffee aren't as impressive, they can still make a difference in your financial reality. If you have an extra $50 per month, just imagine how much interest you could save on credit card debt or your car loan.

Cooking for Yourself Saves More Money

Takeout and delivery have become more than occasional treats. With the huge selection of interesting meal options in most locations, more families opt for convenience rather than cost savings. Not only is it much easier to tap your app for delivery, it also saves you a lot of time that is taken up by other pursuits in today's modern lifestyle. Time is money but spending money to save a little bit of time can wreak havoc on your overall budget. First, recognize that you pay for the food, a delivery charge, taxes on restaurant meals, and still have to give a tip to the driver. The average meal ends up costing two or more times what it could if you cook it at home. Is an extra half hour in your day really worth all that?

Saving Money While Saving Time

If convenience is the major draw of take-out food, consider and freezing individual portions as an alternative. Look up recipes to re-create your favorite restaurant meals and get creative in your own kitchen. From food to almost any other expense, buying base ingredients or parts and using your own skills and energy to create the final thing makes significantly more financial sense.

Brown Bag It – A Delicious and Frugal Solution

One of the major convenience foods or take out draws is lunchtime. You want to get out of your office or other workplace for a break halfway through the day and all your coworkers are heading to the deli, fast food joint or food truck. Meals are social so you might want to join them, but bringing your own food still gives you plenty of opportunity to chat and laugh with people you see every day. A $5.00 sandwich could cost less than $2.00 if you make it at home and bring it with you. If you save $3.00 every day, it adds up to approximately $60 per month if you usually buy only on workdays. Would that amount pay your cell phone bill, pay off your credit card debt months faster or cover your daughter's dance class? Over the course of your adult life, it can add up to nearly $30,000 extra for retirement.

You get the added savings of healthcare costs if you cook your lunch at home. A lot of restaurant and take-out food has high sodium, high fat content and potentially unhealthy additives. Why not buy fresh food at the grocery store, put together your own meals, and minimize the risk of paying for doctor's visits down the road?

Convenience Store Purchases Cost You More

Food is just one item on the budget list where you can save a lot of money with smarter choices. A large part of shifting your personal finance mindset is changing where you shop for everything. This idea covers everything from brand names versus generics, specialty boutiques versus big-box stores, and supermarkets and discount shops versus convenience stores. The Quik Stop attached to your local gas station or the 7-11 down the street makes it easy to stop in, grab a few things and get on your way again in minutes.

These represent another way that time equals money when it comes to creating and sticking to a smart budget. Gas stations earn very little profit on fuel. Convenience stores do not have the option of offering a huge selection of products to earn an overall profit. Instead these venues rely on you making impulse purchases at high markups. You might get cheap coffee, but the breakfast sandwich, bag of chips, wiper fluid, or sunglasses will cost a lot more than they would if you bought them elsewhere. You need to train yourself to resist buying things just because you notice them. These smaller shops boost sales through clever marketing, eye-catching displays, and special offers that look great but rarely save you money. Plan in advance and shop in the sales for car accessories, snack food. Get used to delayed gratification when it comes to making purchases.

Smart Shopping Tips to Save More

A large part of changing your financial future involves everyday decisions that make small differences. Creating a budget, paying off your debt and getting great interest rates on a mortgage may seem more important, but your approach to shopping at the grocery store, mall or online also contribute to true freedom from financial worry. These smart shopping tips maximize savings so you can make more important choices with your money.

Stop Impulse Buying Completely

Nothing busts your budget more quickly than buying things without thinking about it first. Both real-world stores and e-commerce shops are designed to push impulse buy products on you at every turn. No matter how attractive the offers are, what discounts the companies offer, and how much you really want a brand-new this or that, making impulse purchases is the worst thing possible for smart money management.

Somehow you must resist the carefully constructed pull of consumption culture and only buy things you plan to buy. Do not use material acquisition to feel better about yourself, a source of entertainment or a reward for accomplishing anything in other parts of your life. People even become addicted to the rush of buying something new.

How Do You Resist These Shopping Impulses?

Above all else, plan before you shop for anything and stay focused on your specific goal. These tips can help:

- Write down exactly what you need to buy before you start shopping.

- Do not use window shopping as a form of entertainment.
- Never go grocery shopping when you are hungry.
- Plan purchases beforehand to match coupons, sales, and opportunities.
- Resist good deals that you don't really need.

How many times have you purchased a new game, piece of clothing, or household gadget just because it was on a great sale and you felt like you could not pass up the bargain? The savings mean nothing if you never use it.

Cash Back, Points and Gift Card Opportunities

If you are like many people on Earth, more often than not you shop online. With sales and coupons around for specific e-commerce websites, you can also find amazing opportunities for getting free money or rewards every time you spend anything. Cashback or point earning platforms are free to join and give you some type of reward whenever you buy products or services at their partner stores.

How Does the Earning Process Work?

- Log in to the cashback shopping portal.
- Click on the e-commerce store you want to buy something from.
- Shop for the products and complete your order.

- Earn a small percentage of the total purchase price or related points.
- Cash out at a minimum balance or trade points in for gift cards.

While this process will not make you rich, it does make things cost less and rewards you for smart purchase decisions. Not making the most of free money on the table is a bad decision all around.

Use All Gift Card Money

Gift cards and certificates have become a popular reward, present and benefit for occasions such as a birthday or a work bonus. Statistical research has found that hundreds of millions of dollars on unclaimed gift cards are wasted every year. People forget a gift card exists, accidentally throw it out or use only part of it. Many people also wait too long, and the gift card expires.

A large part of shifting your mindset about personal finance must focus on using all free money that comes your way. Gifts are meant to be enjoyed, plus you deserve the reward for staying late at work to help with a big project! Most gift cards have expiration dates printed on them or a toll-free phone number to call to check the balance and other information.

Use the gift card right away. Even if you aren't a regular customer of the company, investigate whether it is worth your while to do so. For example, if you get a restaurant gift card, you can treat yourself to an evening out without any guilt about going over your budget. If you truly cannot use the gift card, consider swapping it with someone else for cash or another valuable item.

Membership, Loyalty, and Discount Cards

Many supermarkets, drugstores, and similar shops offer free loyalty cards to all customers. Under the guise of joining a special membership club, you can take advantage of discounts, special offers, and digital coupons with a simple swipe of your barcode. Online shops have similar opportunities in the forms of coupon codes and rewards programs.

Sign up for as many of these loyalty cards as you can. Use them every single time you go to the store even if you do not think you bought something with a related discount that day. Keep track of special offers and put them on your shopping calendar to maximize savings. Also, check out cumulative reward programs that give you products in return after you have spent a certain amount of money. These are exceptionally popular at supermarkets around major holidays. For example, if you spend $200 in the month of November, you can earn a free turkey for Thanksgiving.

Far too many people miss out on these types of savings because they simply do not remember to take out their key fob or card at the checkout counter. This is where rebooting your thinking comes into play. Once you train yourself to always shop consciously, swiping your card becomes second nature. It only takes a few seconds to do, and the savings add up over time. To make the habit even stronger, take a few minutes after the shopping trip to look over your receipt, add up everything you saved and move that money immediately into a savings account.

Thrift Store Shopping and Second-hand Goods

Manufacturing and mass production have taken over the world in response to the global call of consumer culture. Buying things has become so simple that all you need is a quick swipe or tap on an electronic gadget to spend money, getting everything from food to clothing to cars delivered directly to your home. The quest for new things is destroying not only the natural environment of the world but also your personal financial future.

Buy Used Everything

Other than products with hygiene issues like personal care equipment or underwear, you can buy everything used, preowned, or secondhand with ease. Rather than giving in to the throw-away society, take control of your money and consumption levels by looking for other options first. Thrift stores not only provide a safe source of quality goods, they also support charities for the impoverished, homeless, and other disadvantaged people. You can find name brand clothing for a fraction of the price, tons of toys and games for your children, and household gadgets that work perfectly. Yard sales and garage sales offer even lower prices in most cases. Become a smart shopper and buy based on your needs rather than falling for seemingly amazing bargains. The online world offers similar marketplaces like eBay, Facebook Marketplace or Craigslist. One of the wisest savings decisions you can make is buying a used car. Why spend $30,000 on a new sedan that will be worth half as much the moment you drive off the lot when you could spend $15,000 on a two or three-year-old car that will still last for many years to come?

Brand Names Do Not Mean Higher Value

In some cases, a specific brand name does equal better quality. It is okay to be loyal to some brands if they truly provide value to your life. However, the lure of brand name goods usually has more to do with status than it does with usefulness or quality. Making wise purchase decisions means spending only what is necessary to get the most value out of the product. For example, a well-known brand for rugged work clothing costs more than poorly made outfits from a discount shop. Because you need your work clothes to last a long time and protect you from job-related issues, it makes sense to pay more.

What Doesn't Add Value to the Product?

A focus on true worth is a large part of the mental shift from living paycheck to paycheck to being in complete control of your financial future. No matter what the product in question is, the following things add no value to it whatsoever:

- Fancy packaging
- Clever marketing campaigns
- Celebrity endorsements
- Anything that you specifically will never use

The next time you are in a store or shopping online, compare the ingredients for something like a pain-relieving medication or a can of soup. Chances are the well-known brand name will contain exactly the same ingredients as the generic option and in most cases, the ingredients are likely to have been processed at the same plant. The only difference is the addition of a different label and price before shipping them to the stores.

Save More with Low Unit Prices

A smaller package may have a lower upfront cost, but there is nothing fun about "fun size" when it comes to your budget. The same thing goes for "travel size" bottles of shampoo or tubes of toothpaste. To buy anywhere near enough to last a week or month, you will need numerous tiny bottles. Not only does this introduce more unnecessary plastic and other packaging into the environment, it also wastes your hard-earned money. To counteract this problem, many budget gurus suggest you reach for the largest package possible. This, they say, is where the savings are. However, blindly buying a different size just because someone tells you to is not a smart way to manage your money. Reboot the entire purchasing process by shopping smart instead of making knee-jerk decisions.

Unit Prices to the Rescue

Every item in a supermarket or online store has a unit price listed on the label or product page. This number shows you how much one unit of the product costs. For example, your shampoo may be $0.20 per ounce, making a 16-ounce bottle cost $3.20. If you buy the travel size 2-ounce bottle, you may expect it to cost $0.40. However, in most cases, it will cost a dollar or more. The giant 48-ounce shampoo bottle would come in at $9.60 if the unit price was the same. However, it will usually cost less than that because the per-unit price is less.

Stores know that "buy the biggest package" has been drilled into consumer's heads for a long time. To make more money for their company, they tend to avoid putting the smallest unit price on the largest package. Simply check the label and make a smart decision for yourself. This especially applies to specific products on sale. You can save more by purchasing three 16-ounce bottles rather than one 48-ounce bottle in the long run.

The Issue of Bulk Storage

The only time when bulk purchases and large package options do not make sense is when they overrun your at-home storage possibilities. Everyone has seen the jokes about five-gallon buckets of peanut butter from the wholesale club or packs of 48 rolls of toilet paper that simply won't fit in any closet. While there are many options in the average house or apartment for storage (for example under the couch or in the garage or basement), there is no need to buy extra shelving or another freezer just to save a few cents per unit.

Save on Holidays without Being a Grinch

Christmas and birthdays are two annual events that eat away at a budget. They may test even the most frugal budgeter. Much of this comes down to expectations and competition – after all, you may feel guilty if someone buys you a $100 gift and you give them one that's worth $20. If your neighbors' child has a birthday bash with a petting zoo, inflatable bounce house and catering, your kid may feel left out if all they get is pizza and ice cream. For gift-giving holidays, consider a "Secret Santa" plan or simply buy for less people, or focus on giving homemade or service-related items like car detailing or gardening work. It is quite easy to come up with an impressive holiday or birthday plan without spending thousands or even hundreds of dollars.

Forget Paying for Entertainment Media

Firstly, this is not an invitation to pirate games, steal e-books or plug into your neighbor's cable connection so you can watch the latest show on HBO... When you make a mental shift to a savings-friendly way of life, it should not compromise your morals or make you break the law. However, you can find an awful lot of free entertainment both on and offline. One of the best ways to access free fun is to get a library card; not only can you find a huge number of books there, most also carry movies, music and even video games to borrow. With interlibrary loans and e-book collectives, you may never run out of things to enjoy.

Movies and TV Shows

You can stream practically anything online these days, and that includes both classic and new movies and past and current TV shows. The average cable TV bill in the United States is $107 per month. If you add on the premium channels, the price goes up very quickly. Consider a Netflix or Hulu subscription for less than $20 each, or one of the many free channels available on smart TVs and systems like Roku and Amazon Fire.

Books and Magazines

E-books always cost less than print and you can find a huge variety of free options in every genre possible. It is more difficult to find traditional magazines at super low prices but most websites offer similar information and are simple to access from any Internet or phone connection.

Phones and Digital Connectivity

All of the industries that offer electronics or digital gadgets, especially smartphones, update their offerings on a frequent basis. Every year sees a new, upgraded phone on the market for the top brands. The Internet and late-night television are full of infomercials about the hottest new kitchen gadget or tool to make your life so much easier. The small changes made to existing products combined with clever marketing push the impulse buy habit into the stratosphere.

When it comes to phones, smart technology, and computers, first ask yourself how connected you need to be. Then ask if your existing tech fulfills that need for you. Are you genuinely missing something that would make your life better? Finally, is the cost for that upgrade worth the improvement you will receive for it?

You are not obsolete just because you do not have a few more megapixels for your digital camera, two more megabytes of RAM or a slightly faster processor speed. Companies introduce these things to encourage people to spend more money. Unless you are a professional photographer or videographer, graphic designer or e-gaming superstar, these incremental improvements will provide no additional value to your tech experience. The smart gadget industry is experiencing massive growth. Using your phone, you can now change your thermostat, turn on your lights, lock your doors or talk to your pet dog from your office or while riding the bus. You can schedule almost everything to start automatically. Not only are most of these things unnecessary, they can also lead to higher electric bills over time.

Kitchen and Household Gadgets

All the above considerations go double for kitchen and household gadgets. These products, which are frequently sold online or through long TV commercials with celebrity endorsements, usually offer nothing new when it comes to cooking, cleaning or other aspects of your everyday life.

Look in your kitchen or wherever you keep your cleaning gear. How many of the products or gadgets have you used in the past three months? Is there anything there that you spend money on but have only used once or twice? Getting a new version will not increase its usefulness. The only thing that matters in your new way of thinking about personal finance is whether an expenditure or investment provides sufficient value to make it worth your while. A high-tech mop or digital slow cooker cannot provide any more than an old-fashioned mop or the cooker you have already used for five years.

Changing your attitude about all types of shopping does more for your overall budget than anything else. However, you may wonder if these new ideas focus on frugal living at the expense of fun. Almost everything you currently do and enjoy can fit into your budget with a few smart changes.

Fitness for Both Body and Finances

Of all the things you can invest in and make a part of your regular monthly budget, it seems like health should be at the top of the list. After all, eating healthy food and exercising not only help you thrive and feel great, but can also save you money on medical care in the long run. This investment, however, does not have to equal a whole bunch of money. Take a look at gym membership costs; you can pay $100 a month for a full frills option, or as little as $20 a month for basic equipment and services. Cheaper options also include the YMCA and fitness centers connected to your work.

Do You Actually Use the Facilities?

If you decide to pay for a gym membership, make sure you could cancel it if you stopped going. The best deal means nothing if you must lock yourself into a year's worth of payments when you stop going in February.

Buying Exercise Equipment for Home

Consider preowned exercise equipment, but make sure it is in excellent condition before you buy it. To save even more money, use your own bodyweight or things you have around the house to get fit. Good, old-fashioned push-ups, crunches, squats and lunges go a long way and you do not need to spend a cent. In the United States, healthcare costs a lot; in fact, it is the one expense that bankrupts people more often than any other. Staying fit helps avoid some of these charges, yet you don't need to spend a lot of money to get the benefits. Something as simple as a walk in the park, a regular habit of following calisthenics or yoga videos online or involvement with a fun sports team with a group of friends can get you great results.

Break Addictions and Minimize Vices

When it comes to wasted money, nothing is worse than completely unnecessary and usually unhealthy addictions and vices. The average cost of a pack of cigarettes is over $6.00. At a pack a day, you will waste $180 every single month or over $2000 in a year. Do you have credit card debt or want to save up for a new car? Just imagine how much quicker you will reach your goal with an extra $180. Regular alcohol consumption is another big way to waste money. A six-pack of beer cost about the same as that pack of cigarettes. Addictions need treatment and help to overcome, and that is something worth spending some money on. However, casual drinkers can still change your habits to save money too.

Make Socializing More Affordable

The idea of shifting your thought process about personal finance does not mean giving up every leisure activity or social interaction. You do not have to stay home every time your buddies go out to the bar. The main goal is to make conscious decisions that positively affect your overall financial position. It is simple to say that you should spend less on going out to clubs, eating at restaurants, and visiting special events with friends and family. However, you do not want to give up your entire social life or change your group of friends just because you want to save money. If you can get them on board with more affordable options, great!

Simple Tips to Make Nights out Budget-Friendly

Other than staying at home, there are several things you can do to fit more entertainment and fun events into your new personal finance plan:

- Set a limit on number of events per month
- Choose options that cost less up front
- Buy cheaper drinks, food, tickets, or souvenirs (or none at all)
- Look for discount days or happy hour deals
- Never split the bill – get your own and only pay for what you drink or eat

Frugal Options for Fun and Personal Care

Every person who reads this book undoubtedly has a list of other things they spend money on that they do not want to give up. Perhaps you have a favorite hobby that takes part of your paycheck every month. Maybe you are saving up for a special event that traditionally costs a lot like a vacation or a wedding. It could be that you think there is no way to save on important things like exercise, beauty care, and health food. With the right mindset, you can make frugal decisions that do not compromise your enjoyment of life.

Spending Decisions for Your Wedding

In the United States, the average cost of a wedding is $34,000 and that doesn't even include the wedding rings or honeymoon. That amount of money can buy you a brand-new car (although you should always buy used), a full year of a quality university education or a great down payment on a reasonably priced house.

The day you get married is supposed to be a once-in-a-lifetime event. It is something you will remember forever, and you want to make all those memories great. In the end, most of these wonderful memories will be the actual wedding ceremony and spending time with family and friends. Premium roses instead of standard, or smoked salmon instead of a delicious chicken dish, will not matter one bit when you look back in years gone by.

Tons of Ways to Save on a Wedding

The most important way to use your new smart-money mindset for special events like this to set a budget and stick to it. Get family and friends to help search for bargains or create decorations or food themselves. Will you be happy with quality videos and candid photos, with a few staged shots, or do you need a full Hollywood movie production that you may never watch again?

Saving on a wedding is a great way to start off a life of combined finances. Before you walk down the aisle, you and your partner should have discussed attitudes toward spending and budgeting in depth. This should make it simple to agree on choosing less expensive options for a one-day party.

Beauty Products and Appearances

If you use nothing other than simple soap, toothpaste, deodorant and similar essentials, you will save tons of money on your monthly budget. However, while basic hygiene is acceptable, there is no reason to go cold turkey on your beauty or appearance regimen just because you want to balance your personal budget. Looking your best helps you feel good about yourself and can increase confidence. It can help in your career and personal life too.

The Shift to Less Focus on the Surface

A large part of rethinking finances means shifting your priorities; forget about buying Gucci T-shirts when you can get the same wear out of one from Old Navy. Buying the most expensive makeup, fragrances or cosmetic services does not always get you the best results. The $200-an-ounce beauty cream will not stop the passage of time any more than the $20 one. Your surface appearance still matters, but you can get similar results for less.

Smart Purchase Decisions to Look Your Best

Remember the important rules of purchasing products and services:

- Do not pay for things you do not use.
- Do not buy items with expensive packaging or celebrity endorsements.
- Do not pay more for product with a less expensive one does the same thing.

Savings on skin cream, hair tonic or make up can add up. Saving money on cosmetic procedures like dental veneers, Botox or more extensive plastic surgery usually comes by deciding not to get it done. Decide what makes the most sense for you.

Hobbies – Saving Money on Favorite Pastimes

Some hobbies offer more frugal options than others, but all of them require some expense on materials or gear necessary to take part. If you enjoy knitting, you need to spend money on needles and yarn. If you prefer wilderness exploration, you need a strong pair of boots, a backpack and safety gear. Even simple hobbies like reading still involve some expenses. Hobbies provide entertainment and personal fulfillment and that is worth some adjustments to your budget. They are not intrinsic needs like food, shelter, or utilities; they fit far down in your financial plan. If money is tight or you have a high debt load, you may have to readjust your participation in various hobbies until you get a better handle on your finances. There are two ways to cut expenses and still have fun.

Try New Hobbies or Pastimes

Learning new things provides mental stimulation and a great sense of accomplishment. Try new hobby that does not cost as much as one you already enjoy. You may be able to find free classes at a local craft store or community college. You can always find free tutorials and video lessons online. Consider hobbies that make use of found materials or upcycling things you already own. Trash to treasure can offer great rewards and potentially be a way to make money if you sell the goods you create.

Save on Your Favorite Hobbies

No matter what you do in your free time, you can undoubtedly find a way to save money on it. This is more difficult if you are competitive cyclist, downhill skier or love rebuilding classic cars – these activities have higher price points than drawing, needlework, or stamp collecting.

Where appropriate and possible, buy preowned gear. A mountain bike owned by someone who gave up on the pastime after a few months will work just as well is one brand-new from the shop. The same goes for things like painting easels, wood carving tools and soldering irons. Shop thrift stores, yard sales and online marketplaces for everything else. Also, consider monetizing your hobby and earning money to put back into it. You can sell handmade goods online or at craft shows and flea markets. This is a great way to take part in your favorite pastime without cutting into your budget at all.

Congratulations

Now that you have finished this book, you should have a strong understanding of what it takes to reboot your thinking and gain control over your personal finances. It all starts with creating a budget so you know where your money comes from and where it goes. Then, each regular expense, individual purchase or financial decision needs appropriate attention and care so you don't fall into the traps of paycheck-to-paycheck existence or debt.

Financial comfort and success come down to just a few essential changes:

1 – Make a budget and keep track of everything so you stay informed about your financial reality.

2 – Pay for needs before you even think about wants. Minimize these expenses like rent, utility bills, and grocery shopping as much as possible.

3 – Get rid of debt as quickly as possible. Pay off high interest loans first, make more than the minimum payments and snowball payments until you are free.

4 – Use all possible discounts, cashback or point-earning opportunities, and shop sales for everything. Comparison shop for products and services every time.

5 – Eradicate all impulse buying. Ask yourself if you need the product or service, if you will use it regularly, and how much value it will bring to your life?

6 – Let go of materialistic ideas that focus on appearances and personal value tied to how much money you have or the brand names of product you use. Think practically and spend money on items and experiences that truly add value to your life.

www.ingramcontent.com/pod-product-compliance
Lightning Source LLC
Chambersburg PA
CBHW071417210526
45465CB00001B/438